CITY OF CORNERS

Books by John Godfrey:

26 Poems (Adventures in Poetry, 1971)

Three Poems (Bouwerie Editions, 1973)

Music of the Curbs (Adventures in Poetry, 1976)

Dabble: Poems 1966-1980 (Full Court Press, 1982)

Where the Weather Suits My Clothes (Z Press, 1984)

Midnight On Your Left (The Figures, 1988)

Push the Mule (The Figures, 2001)

Private Lemonade (Adventures in Poetry, 2003)

JOHN GODFREY

CITY OF CORNERS

WAVE BOOKS
Seattle • New York

Published by Wave Books
www.wavepoetry.com

Wave Books titles are distributed to the trade by
Consortium Book Sales and Distribution
Phone: 800-283-3572 / SAN 631-760X

Library of Congress Cataloging-in-Publication Data
Godfrey, John, 1945-
  City of corners / John Godfrey. — 1st ed.
      p. cm.
  ISBN 978-1-933517-32-2 (alk. paper) -- ISBN
978-1-933517-31-5 (pbk. : alk. paper)
  I. Title.
  PS3557.O29C58 2008
  811'.54--dc22

                              2008012112

Thanks to the editors of the journals who have published
some of these poems: *Bald Ego, Hanging Loose, Kulture Vulture,
Sal Mimeo,* and *Shiny.*

Designed and composed by J. Johnson
Printed in the United States of America

9 8 7 6 5 4 3 2 1

FIRST EDITION

Wave Books 015

CONTENTS

WAITING THERE

And you go down that street
Rainbows ahead bling you
like midnight never does
and I wonder where
evening will be tonight
My loved ones waiting there

I pretend my swagger
through debris
is the holy dance
of the many my days
On the remotest sidewalk
facing the moon
I cannot say
the orphan still lives
and you recognize
the battleground
You can hide her in
quadrangle dirt
The buildings are
old and half blind

With an enemy
like daylight who needs
the psychology dime
Hips do the work
and I cross the world

DEPENDS

Depends how energetic your pity is
How the screwball you are differs
from the one you trust
Venerable ones bump my past
I am grateful for the tarmac curb to curb
Puddles shine there with the texture of silk

The circle around her right eye
and the rare engine in her cheekbone
To her left swings hang broke in harmony
It is the moment per day for a mild riff
You realize it in a hand open and stiff
Pattern of light on the verge of rupture

You corner the market on bowls of hands
You learn from the indecency of others
and progress to a rewarding dissonance
You tug on her skirt when he shows up

The message was her makeup
Fluorescent tends to impoverish the look
until you realize the container
is dark velvet brown

COMES WITH GALORE

Dabs of light on the pocket
Oblivion is always legal
Hey, you know, there
are sweet accidents and
hair with unearthly sheen
Stand aside for the keel of litter

There never were any heroic marbles
They stifle everything that hard
Even stone rings of fragility
It is plenty they attend to
and the perversion of taste
that comes with galore

Mercurial responses then splat
Brilliance at a mere simmer
while she considers her odds
As chance has it they are infinite
She sees herself scurry and hide
She claps an eye before white lines
and lives on up close
to where the beautiful king

ALL THE HAIR

Snow weeps jewels on trash
Can't sleep nights in that dream
You approach as arpeggio

Murder arouses ministrations
But I have reverent lips
Always you follow a form of child

You and less than you
All the hair is the question
More time than I figure

I hope only a little bit
I had better not help you
Smoke rolls down the street

It makes no mind if it's real
It is I who begs to differ
You are only mostly you

LANCE

Exit the walk-in closet of air
Bold colors where was luminous mist
The jinx, you think, is behind you
Nausea and bad temper too
Bagman inside makes his last drop
He is in ruthless pursuit of bread soup
A choir of the cheerless garnish the trudge
Tongues and souls parched on elevators
Caught in the daytime net cast by bricks
Fleece of the brain snarls out of eligibility
Dream of jailbreak and the escape bike
Clinging to the belly of a black sheep
Woeful return to society with fleece of tar
You score a point for every place you've seen
A particular emphasis on doubt
It should clasp me like the lover I sleep
with but never wake up to, rippling
the shoulder knot of my goad
The idea of a rematch is repugnant
The template of a theft escapes
On the sidewalk the powdered shape of a man
In the backseat a lance with fiber and blood
The edge is keen and hearing keener
You choose the dead cinch
You count precisely nicked coins
Every now and then pause for a nip
The heartless appear in a flattering light
Never slow for bumps

SLIDE

Weapons pose the problem downstairs
Excrescences agreed upon
You wait all this time for dew

Good morning, unindustrialized
                    clouds
Riff–length communion
                    Slide

Stirrings grayly lit, blankets askew
Drizzle finds the steps
Odors fertilize joy

I don't see a clearing take place
                    Dank
Must find the source of your scent
                    Dream

EACH HAIR

Extend the fuse an inch
Sometimes they kneel here
They'll never know

Richer yellows emerge
Snow blinds for a second
Feel each hair blown straight

Can't resist opportunity
Change swaddled just so
A lot of sensible denials

Wary and flatfoot
Ice you can't melt
I'm talking about you

The vein is exhausted
Press back on the wind
Lips not fit to kiss

THE DEADPAN

The ripe and the mature alike
Wry smile suggests latent hate
One beckons wildly for something to happen
A certain rhythmic trot
From car to bus to queue
Scapular medallion bears her name
I squint to read it
A certain sting to have forgot it once
and I slop watery coffee on a defective shoe
The deadpan was taught to her in infancy
That many days to whittle down to
Her parlor manners are a little different
Now and then a bootleg smile
when the overconfident strike out
She throws a split glance past him
The elevator she draws upward with her
past yellow teeth and shoes on doorsills
Gadfly poses interruptions where
the inside and the outside corners overlap
The path she has chosen treads to a window
Things they hurl at the indigent
She is so very far from the scramble
Others in line are equally proud
They have known the night of lice
Stewed the bark of saplings and
know when to step out of the shadows

STARLING

Leaves the car wash
No no no no
She wins that round
Reservations procured
Soap suds on open shoe
Like a starling in sunlight

Essence applied to neck
Don't wait for modifications
No lipstick on filter
Blonde to detonate delicacy
Slide off the stool just so
Playacting out of fairness

Contributions unenumerated
Purse always in hand
Plate glass mirror by streetlight
Person intent to be in place
Dialogue not yet occurred to her
Now the stage is upset

Follow equals wander
Perhaps her empty secret
I'm no good at others' integrity
She seems to wait for me
Left no other choice
We cross with the light

CONVENIENCE

Come out now they are gone
One engine I think leaves twice
Somebody must be the other

So calm so aware
Unity is entire, you detect
a convenience where you'd expect

No less than one can be
a witness in doorway
Punch to arm along directly

All because I want her any cost
Dissemble and negotiate
Curve rolls over body

Require breath in identical ways
Diverge because it is hip
Do not save changes

THE PARTICLES

Harsh and pitiless currents tumble
You mistake the latent for decay
Then one day all it takes
A mild extended light
The malice of hope in yellowish green
A dozen queue guys call "Tock-say!"
You can say that's justice or germane

The erasure differs from silence
Not to hear your name called
Hear it only as a practicality
You can't correct the longing
You want to hear it expressed
Sheet over window for adequate dark
Nothing over a still, long leg

To listen everything's equally real
Acceptable only as another question
To build elasticity of morals
Unable to live up to
your scruplelessness
Events fly in the face of ingenuity
Clutter in the descent from birds
Reconstitute suspension of self
I notice the skin between breasts

Submission to the endless dawn
Shouldn't feel this sharp
Night and day, any light can teach
In fog fluorescence penetrates
My wants multiply the particles

Those of us who pass through earth
As if vegetation celebrates a brutal woman

Flares, flashes, three on a match
Natural light has nothing to do
Between *is* and *ought* expanse of biddings
Almost is always the first time
Your palm supports my jaw
Your belly in half-light
The end of everything

Wish a star to stay where it is
Less anger than exhibitionism
Doorway constantly occupied
Marijuana in special linen
What is it she's got anyway
The voice I never hear
Exclusive dress protects from light

Layer on layer confounds me
Hear my nerve grate against teeth
What I don't want resolves
I get harmony as what I want
No order this derives from
Gymnastics of personality
To take my arm you can't tell

Reprise the anodyne gag
In sunlight faint brunette in her hair
Fine hand larger than mine
What she considers decorum
Electrified salts of her body
Gust conforms her clothing
When she walks she rides

ON THE PLATFORM

No more than what I find
Skin beyond brown
All of a piece

This time call it shade
Open backed with flanks in motion
Looking for her Metro card

On the platform call it shadow
Half-naked nonentity
Nipples in a/c car

Every word repossession
Big-ticket item
Kiss on the mouth

A THORN

Brother to dust
Carries a thorn
with his foot
Gets kicks between
a woman's fingers
Absolves the putrid mass
he inherits
When I too
we'll see how brave
More across
than opposite
More than ten
hands high

The wreckage is lost
without you
Where the color
of your palms meets
the backs of your hands
You do not know
that I escape
into space for you

IN THE CLOUDS

Qualities daylight lacks
Decaled nail against her eyetooth
Grin of wile, razor next to weave kit
Unpredictable patience
One step per second
and they say she's gone
I see in the forecast
a face not beautiful when still

Opening in the clouds
Pecking order of stars
Where the voluntary orb
Down here ablution by dust
and the smoke of cessation
What to do
Toothbrush in my wallet
Put a blanket on
the party of the first part
Look so good up in my face
Backward on the balls
of her feet
Sad insistence
Glory in her pocket

HANG BETTER

Improbable frisson
Quiet murderer
      Chains link a fence
      Trash grills there
You are standing
      dead center
Anybody moves and it's
sudden allover steam

You loosen the rope
You hang better
      across her back
Behind it all
the cornucopia
      The million ways
events appear
Your importance
      owes everything

BEAT IT

Something happens alright
Anatomical luxury
My body your body tattoos
Rafaelo aka Ralphie says
nobody knows but Lupe
Gets you a sixth-floor window

So alive I forget to beat it
I turn longing into admiration
I could sleep in a curbside
excavation but I don't want to
There is no more meaning in
the responses of others

I point out to you
that I breathe
Instructions always incomplete
Give me that mood crap
And this will always haunt you

CRADLE

Optical reaction on a big scale
Every color habitually matte turned glossy
Fool'd have words with that chartreuse
Abundance of mean things under the brush
Even my demons shine as if spit on
Something green about the surfeit
Outsider insinuate the flesh tones of privation
Noble ones resist, succeed, and pander
Never have colors so unmasked tidiness

Impulses chafe and become brittle
Clap of thunder herds the one-armed
Depravity compares well to contagion
Anatomy deflates upon its ideals
Ravages denied to the degree they're untamed
To use denuded land to sour the blood
The wild girl offers you her card
and the brown waters of her skin become fluent

When I stand in the cradle of blasphemy
Ambrosian tongue of flame degrades exposure
With no effort I admit ballast
to the stage peopled with clowns and thugs
I can dig how some grasp life as a swap meet
But my chains lack that link
I watch a hand convert a child's forehead
The curl of a rind in sunlight
Lower eyelid hovers above a blue shadow
I am the only one left to consume

SILHOUETTE

Weary excuse for doom
Sparkle on oiled brown forehead
Rising sun bustles from girl to girl
Spills tones of luck on lack
Lonely woman theme gone solo
Mad skimpy and tight's a sight
Untimely floss on appointment day
with a bow to the night from a runaway
Verizon relay on a belt
in touch with obstacle number one
Variations on implore and spite
Looks alone make a man dizzy
Elaborate a history of affection
drawn from kitchen living bed and death room
Hope out on bail for all my effort
My relations are dying, got that under my feet
Dreams go on living beyond my means
I can't understand how discipline
is of any concern to the annihilated
Depends on what she considers survival
as she dodges calamity
Silhouette her hard face on the wall

A SELECTION

What many despise
At its most horizontal
sunlight smears damage

I can only respond
with a selection

To think to be
a janitor of perceptions
Sidewalk factually cleaner
Scorn magnifies in plain sight
intermittently militant
Where the faces
overwhelm me

Accounting consists of change
Can't look on it always
Suddenly control my hands
Bleakness flows in wind
Really something there

STRAINING TO HEAR

You so livingly glance
Dirt again yields bud
Satisfy me that you
have salami grease chin
The sun pretends to pull
more than just so
I enter the penetrating sight

Brevity affects the skin
Wherever I sleep foam pillows
Blackout windows night before
Crumbs, sugar grains, comedy
Sun's retreat to window box
Can't remember love in May
Nipple hardens in twilight chill

Sleep larger than life
Softness is not meant for you
Hair blown forward then back
Straining to hear over car radio
The smallest unit of knowledge
Aftertaste of rosewater
Weight of the world in my mouth
Sidewalk rises to meet her feet

CITY OF CORNERS

My first trial is hung
The soul battery charge
and the predictive
folded arms
I hear nothing
That's what they say

The malady though
It ruminates from
the gut and
one hand fractionally
anticipates the other

So my defense is love
for a city of corners
you disappear around
and inside I die

FLOSS AT THE BARBECUE

You walk toward me
No you don't
Had me fooled
Standard deviation to elevate
lingerie to beachwear
Chemise to uncompromising
floss at the barbecue
Cheek not smooth and
your dark presentation
Speaks first words softly
Well-understood coyness
for her to be
living on high
Bewildered, distract myself
Don't expect that heavy voice
At the sound a few
shift in their chairs
Spoons rock against crockery
She repeats herself
I follow her to the limits
of my eyes
Subject to evacuations
I imagine details of
light housekeeping
What are her shows
How often she balls
What she is so used to
it is truth

ROOFTOPS BEGIN

Everywhere I go
they're all over the floor
Nipples indurated
under thick wool
What you gonna do
when the lights go up
I won't go unless
you stay here
Lipstick trace on my memory
Every lip
mingles the taste

Where clouds leave off
and rooftops begin
I want you to know
features from trailers
Cold whistles
between high heels
Leads to the red alert
on the rest of the moon

LOOPS

Burden of cloud so calm
Mess completely exculpatory
Maybe you prefer dry twenties

How does Saturday go
Smoke loops over keyboard
Restless, ignore brilliance

The regal flows of it
The microtones
The furry parts of it

Everyone else leaves
I need you again
Loudness of your heels

109,894

City miles

Brilliantine glare, hatless in sunlight
Gusts of fresh ocean air
Holes drilled through heat
Thousand sounds of "See you, baby"

Shadows protect from emergency
Names unsaid in corners
Whenever women and children shelter
Around the table, no still hands

Anxious momentum of traffic
Yellow ciggie dust interior
Windows wide to unruly conventions
Chain-smoke frustration and concern
Thumb poised near horn button
Investigator of childhood
Car that never hides

THEN HER FACE

Goodwill to connive
Worldly semblances to scale
I hate the divisions
and it is hate
that slaughters illusion
Then her face shines

Fried rice and four wings
That you are inured
is not a priori
Physical inflection
of big ideas
Hips as identity

The word back
in Augusta GA
for Eurydice
Behind the wheel
of the bus
Orphée noir

You got to move

HURT

Bring up her virtues
Damp penetrates lips
Past the second light

Can't get alterations
Kids learn fear in time
Old enough to know who to

Cold and nervous
He becomes hurt
It isn't me doing it

Tell him by knife scars
Reinvest the funeral home
Ain't nothing change

A SMALL FRACTION

Sky a small fraction of daylight
and the girlfriend cries
From what window you
gon' jump when there
ain't no access
Sackcloth and resentment
Only one is contemporary

I had to tell her
It was the only way
to get at them

Fire is the worst of it
Other changes pend
For now I can sleep
with you on all sides

FULL SISTER

Take pride in a full sister
Lay it end to end for a sea mile
Waves lie prone before it
Settle the hair of her head
on the shoulder of my coat

Even a hijacker feels this
It is the aviator in me
seeking out winds

Navigate by the fixed star
Along your course festivity
Proceed without deliberation

Downpour at your heels
Fountains caught by the lights of a car
Power over darkness
Shots of worn brick behind braids:

Young man in dark blue shell

YOUR FROTH

As you proceed the marvels that are forbidden
The one at your elbow dispatches you
With certain reservations you are earthbound
Your voice joins in as they recite fossil lore
You do not want a stake in it
and this is presumed to be hesitation
The amplitude of your froth betrays you
and all they who wait to devour
I put forth my ruddy profile
I feel with my toes for the borderline
Violation upon insult among the retinue
and the vessel of inspiration
with which to attain a hard-on
Darkness sets everything right
and to be useful in reticence
That is the chance you find already taken
Advantage all in anticipation
One regains consciousness not alone and surprised
An auspicious odor dispersed by fan
A body as palpable as any of its names
I suffer the heaviness of her arm
and pretend that she can hear

FIREBALL

A married woman stops and listens
If someone should mistime appreciation
She manages to watch him err
as from her hand drops the rind
No more comment about her purse
Her shadow a ghost of itself
She has lived because she is violent
and the supernatural abandoned her
The fireball behind closed eyes
To rise from the designated plot
Everything she wears looks tumbledown chic
Character of a cork to bob up
Turns her insides to debris
I am the one who retards time
I remove the shoes of the offender
Nothing I can do about the mannish
thing she loves in the accused
Inferior crest of the pubis
She's too beautiful for a guardian
and too potent for a juvenile
Leaves the wrongdoer running
Magician on her left disappears

RELAY

Listen for the tumbler to fall
Dedicate your sensitive fingers to property
You will know when the obeisance is right
Some return from the pyre
Some irremediably yearn for smoke
Thankful at the pole lacking ice
Torrid places nudge damp money in my pocket
This is too palpable to undo and I'd
rather tame nothing about the blue
To be rapt at the moment I withdraw
A pleasure to uproot chaos and replete it
At the bridge where you expect to sigh
and various insights maneuver
The betrayal of hierarchy by diction
All depend on this timely rudeness
Use teeth to destroy a stitch
Only freedom within a woman's breath
Your reverence at best appropriate
Hew from thought what is less than that
The morning is partly new
You dilate the designated eye
Deal with the cinder under its lid
What I relay from my hand to yours
The drain of color and glare

EBB

I open the window and clear air rushes out
My practice embarrasses my prophecy
Particles veer away from me
The junction of compassion and touch
Neon the soft face obstinate
Call long enough and out come the elite

I have scraped together with thieves
I remember incredibly hard nipples
It is sobering to ebb
I bear it all to go on, chance of a whirl
But it's still only a breast
The harm to yourself mild

ACROSS THE WAY

You connect the corners
with footsteps
Portions of the foregoing
steal from the air

Serendipity a plus

Reassuring discomfiture
No, not fate
        Musician
Fretboard prepared
with paper clips
Shadowing one, anomie

Place donation in shade
Across the way, braids glow
in unmarked doorway

Full-term rotundity
in steamy daylight
Her posture:
Magnificent

BATHROOM MIRROR

Heat welcomes
      introspection
Marginate the edgy
      Release perfections
Where you belong
      a ball going on

Wires disappear
      Where you are
Finger traverse air
      anytime
Conditions favor
      the shakedown

Slow down the past
      Move like it
I am underneath
      your clothesline
Feathers in your pillows
      Foggy bathroom mirror

FOUR FEET

At least the table is not set
Nearby short hair, light makeup
Sidewalk empty, four feet
No expectant expression

Curb worn out of the wall
This dust lacks nothing
Moves cigarette from one hand
Recalls the brief conniption

Now I am opposite her
Naked legs are everything
She is not necessarily located
There is food on her lip

Confuse daydream with sleep
Relentlessly screw authority
She likes to have you around
One kiss, things get worse

MEMORABLY LOW

You don't have some time
Pigeon clips shoulder
Phrase like a laser through traffic
This corner's only one of four
Think best watching girls pass
To each his own well

The first time I hold my tongue
How real, touch of leather sleeve
Memorably low yellow light
Close attention defies
Look at cigarette, reply briefly

You call yourself magnetic
Screen in place of circulation
Emphatic right forefinger
You conduct a voodoo march
Martial bearings with sudden smiles
I know about you the *in koey'd*

Streetlight powered by juice
I know I know
That's blood to you

PERILOUS THINGS

Change of equilibrium
Few perilous things
more perilous
Presumably risk
their depreciation

A little self-conscious
Dressed awful low
A look from a woman
Everything will be okay
Too brief, ambiguous

Avenue lifeless
Stagger at a distance
Lots of skin, all colors
Prolix landmarks
Sameness forgiven

Wind tunnels as sun lowers
Hard nipples in B cups
Ecstatic branches whip
Hair in buns, in braids, in hats
refuses to move

INTO THE MURAL

Come back, I need you to bind me
I lose countless necessities
My meager return, to hear good-bye

I yield a body part
Underneath bravado
I prod in futility

Colors scream wrapping hair
and they impress gentility
The more vivid the pawn the more
fate sifts down cosmetic powder

Appearance now plump

A copy of the self in hand
Down to the very last drag
Slip into the mural and weep

PERSUADE

Driving is the easy part
Bleach light from the sky
Your nose your eyes now radiant

So you are losing you didn't know
You are clinging to a way to be used
There are endless similarities to life

Liberty leads but does not guide
You laugh at me with every answer
You demonstrate paradoxical welcome

There's no room in the front seat for this
Rhythmic light through windshield
I desperately want to persuade you

The face without makeup
Objections from every side
You memorized words for times like this

only for use at one tomb

LAST HAIR

The evening ahead extends
a long-fingered hand
Now in darkness on all fours
An endogenous musk
In distant headlights
skin glistens and
what's she know
That an evangel
of nastiness lives
between her and
a sweet by-an'-by
Sound of spike heels
and denims with a bell
All the things a woman
can't change
about her luster

It's inevitable
to imagine the feelings
of the fugitive
Maybe I'm a fool
The sinister lightning
I don't see in time
When she calls my name
Denial clings like down
Demented with great back
Come into the traveling light

Tagged to take away
No one sees at all
I remember everything

you miss, last hair
left on your thigh
Lilt of Southern times
A sequence that does not
flatter and does
not illuminate
Maybe a song

CHILL OFF

And if I don't please
everywhere are doors
Only wait for the dust to alight
The person you desire
to trust is wrong
Wind against windows
augments the specter
Back of my hand pressed
between a thigh and blanket
To start with I
meet you in the sound
wet lips make
Takes the chill off
At the worst nothing
is meant at all

WITH FICTIONS

Protect atonement and debase
that, for instance, girl
Cannot explain the discomfort
Laughter of understanding
Transgression not even a question
Way her neck ascends
All plausible, left with fictions
Pray for youth to succeed
where death in the hallway
leaves off, relief may yet
cost me my life
Rather the young woman ahead
than whom in every way
I am smaller
kill me with a shiver
of her ass and I
perish of my thoughts

PITY

I toke water from the dock
Downstairs millipedes glow
What means quarter moon

So the scum becomes part
Unceremonious beatings
Share of what's going on

There are so many nothings
It seems like little pillows
A pause at no expense

Courage raised by disappointment
Fatherly cold and terrible
Pity on all virgins

DOORSTOPS

Alley serves as a megaphone
No hiding the earnings of ten hours
Her vocabulary turned up to a boil
She *can* still, when she needs to travel light
Restlessness is a sort of payment
for all the moments that fail to transport
The women lining the stairs are biased
and she hides in one palm the gold gaming chip
Never ignore her song and dance
What she needs is a devoted gorilla
who might better read for her
the drunken romantic from the drunken man
At no loss to her eloquence
she riffs on a remote chord
or insightfully the notes soar
She gives up one refuge like it's nothing
for others and then skids into doorstops
Bit by bit forget the ingredients
No apology, some are rare
I want to give her without a frill
She is used to the basin and falling door
In her own way enamored
Easy to fool in the short term
To do this you have to be hollow
Anyone will guess on the avenue
And you will never see your offspring

TISSUES

Rasp of fingers on the strings
Clothes a call to love
She says she's Bijou

You can take someone you need
and despite the eeriness
penetrate her hypothetical hatreds
Exert pressure as a color of skin
to have it right under my nose
Betray her with praise so that
her displeasure ignites
a dream of you as ill-equipped spy
Play at truce so she is mired in haste
She becomes the violator and
enjoys tall tales with the villain

Other kinds of forfeiture have merit
She finds a ribbon unnecessary
She bounces her wrist on an itchy braid
and looks beautiful at a distance
You can be arbitrary with names
because she is credulous and disloyal
She develops without protection
No one speaks of rewards
Did I finish it or did she
smoke it all, stoned and emphatic
I am ashamed of not being fooled
as she strains toward the shallow end
She is in question to others
Good faith without reason
Tissues torn apart

NEARLY PERFECT

Barbarities abound
in sanctified drag
Liquidates the nutrients
Let us dine afloat
past the nearly perfect skin
of I forget her name
You don't have to whistle
The door of cards (the house of)
swings face up against
the wall of numbers
I walk through with you
over scattered kings and queens
Bury them with extreme prejudice

Some peace in the uprising
is not necessarily sound
I want one abuse at a time
dissected over and over
to the rim of equity

I learn the cares of a hairdresser
I see her leave extensions intact
The influence of bangs on
again, nearly perfect skin
Proximal arm is not for her support
The shame that never wants
maybe not in her deep self

Cold moves me on
I expel a moment
of smoke

NEWCOMERS

Out of nowhere wind chimes
Imagine layered cloth napkins
Sleep's garbled translation
      Sinister bonhomie
      of paradise
About all you can
expect of newcomers

Wants you to stick
to your current line
      Wants you
to suck out all the air
from the Sterling Street stop
Notes passed you by the tiger
Insignificant natural light
rakes the momentarily
      abandoned
      sweatshirt

FREE FALL

Years change the housing
Where a raw person goes
Wake up on a different floor
Shame doesn't suit
Memory an accident
Necessity and the next dream
You and your deep doo-doo

Both sisters a trifle nutty
Coupla babies in free fall
Customs that travel badly
Too dark for gray areas
What kind of collateral
Thought slower than it sounds
She merely has to get it out

Just like a reservation
Go ahead, keep the house
Shock as silent persons go by
Not exactly the world's
favorite color at this time
Your beautiful nose and eyes
Always the same — blame

END OF IT

Dismay and disappointment
Follow ubiquitous
silver car

Your keys are
in your pants
in the room

The scope yields
one lit window
No silhouettes

If you return
this time might
be the end of it

Viscous shadow
Four-color night
Don't even think about it

PASSAGEWAYS

Talking to her at the junction
Modest swallow full
Hair woolly and silver
descends from fog
The closest one who
almost knows you
Or else an arid grace
until a slave
Where they forget
your appearance

This is your wishing
Cardboard everything
Completely odorless vapor
Hands so well kept
Finger skin deep brown
and prematurely wrinkled

Dominated by smooth
perfectly curved sheathes
Cheekbones lifting lips
Glacial rise of hairline
I compromise so little
Combative touches to
familiarity

The passageways
The passionate perform
Everything a matter of veils
Pleasure in the disguise
Pieces of cloth to cover her

Smaller and smallest
Details of follicles and
pale glossy hairs
Beautiful proportions
of a large hand
Even daylight relative
Sleep in her excuses

BACKSEAT TALK

Last cloud turns back into bone
Anita's shadow doesn't move either
Few long faces at the wake

Someone gifted hums behind his voice
Cheeks stuffed with batting, she starved
She has a hired ride outside

Devil in the backseat talk
Drastic pressure on the chest
Rain as aerosol in streetlight

Drop you at the A train
Droplets baffle headlights
World shares lightlessness with me

AROUND THE WORLD

Anticipation
        slowly relapses
Look where
        the moon rises
Light gusts
        without chill
Whose luminous
        red hair
No escape from
        this booth
But here I am
        around the world

You grow until
        you get hit
By any chance
        you have a choice
Rebel what how
        when you rise
Matter of
        factamente
so few places
        this skin can't leave

You'll never live
        to see it wither
Same four corners
        waiting for a guy
I throw it before
        I've got it caught
Someday unless

it happens at night
Hair tosses
in the semidark
Nothing left to
say for these times

TREES

Some instances, yes, no flight
Inside deep red cloth weaves
Absorbs you in the end

Day so slow she counts it out
Armpits wet, ends stringy
Shuts down her chips and windows

Hard ride subway at length
Defrost youthful neighbors
Homelight timer on

Feeling her way in sleep
Damp heat clings to face
Relaxed hair across arm

Her tongues include longing
Thought in primary dialect
Through window shadows move

THE ONE WHO TURNS

Loss of reflection
To long to return
Trust in companions
and in their idleness
I cannot be one of those
like whom I most feel
Substantial and bleak
in alien fraternity
Kneading the ball
Clasping the necklace
Turning to the one who turns
toward you half asleep
Complete disregard of attachment
to remember all my life

SWEPT AWAY

I happen just not to be worshipping
lackluster nails and geopolitical hips
The invalids are swept away
and only the spry of many races
pass few by few in the rain
Storefronts are dark in honor of
No One from No Where

Shadows around eyes tell nothing
Her long coat's furry hem
settles to the sidewalk like pearls of bleep
Stable and anxious is a helluva way to be
over where black looks good onya
Palm of the hand large with minute brown lines
Damp clothes Newport odors and pipe stains
Heavy air whips around and duplicates us
Clouds I evade and tars that distill
Uneasy when eyes are too trusting
and the natives who emerge from their sea
lack wires lack nets lack pull
I dream myself large
to overcome the forgetfulness
your death enables and
the fraction of survival

Replenish instruments to divine oblivion
Flame hardly wavers in cupped hands
Smoke rapidly twists to the left
and dissipates before it
reaches your face

SMOOTHEST CHEEK

Okay baby the choir is gone now
Inconvenienced by murder
Silenced by delight
I navigate a planet
other than this one

That star is for dogs
The beat turns the moon
The home to return to
emulsifies style
Still you have the smoothest cheek
Your halter restrains me

You can barter
for lighter skin
You can have
the most pregnant smile

ANY COUNTRY ON EARTH

They are crowded and swirling
They are all white and do not
correspond to any country on earth
Don't think that of me
I'm, like, gratitude to trap sets
I'm   Wonder who you with
        On the comeback
        One night at Flora's
        Anybody and me

I must not be listening
At midnight, strangely, visible
I continue to subordinate everything
to the emergence of bite
You know how helpless
        Don't lift that way
        Box of light on the floor
        Come into its shadow

AT BAY

Not I who seeds the enmity
Wrong things to do on schedule
The "if" accounts for your absence

Car too green for surveillance
A few green children on the footpath
Secrecy diverts their pretend breaths

The light is kind to other faces
She crosses wrists to defy shade
Only attractive women hide to loiter

It is the last thing I ever do
Now I comprehend the dancer's hand
Worn upholstery attends the sublime

It has lived so long with blight
An odor warns me of meanness at bay
Kind enough to be forgettable

Feet burn in oxygen shoes
Keys for every parked car ring
I pass, small lights blink under wheels

THROUGH THE WALL

I forsake your lips
to get in on the action
Then you are gone
and I get along

Direction all I lack
I catch myself in time
Angles all discordant
No way through the wall

I take what I need
Between me and nothing
stands what I want
When that's enough I know

Will you know me
Not at twenty feet
You pass like water
I can always call your star

DON'T REACH

Let gust run through my fingers
Return hand to pocket
        full of singles
Screaming ambulance I don't
mind, widow-y panels of cloth
        Bizarre and accustomed
Lights inside fog drum fingers
Drops suspend from railing
        Ashamed to be a witness
Drawer of the heart, secrets
got your number
Tell the whole world

Endlessly sabotage the endangered
Dreams of her own creation
Illusion so bitter as it begins
Hold close in disbelief
Turn hand over as a signal
Don't nobody look that good
after you, well, look

Table floats in smoke
Feet don't reach barroom tile
Steps lead down from where
sidewalk is an afterthought
And thought, you know, is what
makes it difficult

PUCE SHOE

Social gathering wet street neon highlights
I do not recoil from puce shoe cigarette burn
The guardian is late as are the hosts
Would I could disentangle my breath from this hair
Boos resound from the tournament
The bath in the center of the veranda
I have been to havens worse than this
It has nothing to do with dead reckoning
You are primary and select to take yourself away
Light falls all over one's body as it does yours
Merry or not they await her
now that they have extirpated hecklers
She lifts the curtain of melancholy having folded it
In the reservoir of her ear dissonant chiming notes
How inspired her beauty when you let her get over
I could spend the rest of my life erect
as ashes collect at my fingertips
I grieve my loss of eligibility
now it is impossible to be unconscious
and all the silhouettes through windows so sleek
The pirate who mans the door
Solitaries he admits need a jilt
Indistinct odor of feet and beverage
The monsoon creates advantages
Those who only wish they could vanish
Many the bibulous salute
I spy her through an orchard of smoke
At home in paradise, the part near the zoo

A LITTLE SHREDDED

That sinking feeling has been riddled over enough
One pauses to concoct infatuation out of memories
Like a monkey swinging by its tail
Awareness has a speed less than headlight's
and always how impressive the back of a hand
Another pause in token of a mutual dream
Alas the tenement you cremate in
They were little more than misdemeanors
Failure to unhitch from what's least likely to happen
Results in the hijack of several of your names
All because the sheath clung when you ran
Stream from the funnel overwhelms you
If one is to soothe the lion, perhaps *be* the lion
Morning finds you far removed from the dais
Through the door what you see is not exile
It is a bog where your life will change
How radiant it is as it worsens
until fighting fish give up and dignity returns
An ornament out of some cottage industry
hangs a little shredded from your lamp
You hide everything slovenly there
and you emerge skin dried eyes wet

THE PRICE

She returns for the sake of a girlfriend
Never know from the way she maneuvers her spine
Gold heat waves catch the glow coat
on her back like after she dances
But her morale offers nothing to see
Fists of hot air cuff her in multiples
Makes her psych out and in
to where the tenderness excruciates
Glare off her sweat strikes amber in her iris
It seems possible I am the hostage
but then history boils egregiously
The way not to behave on that corner
of the park, taking leave as a message
Shallow and infrequent breaths
What are you willing to do on a bus
Mouth words over your shoulder
Watch your hips roll, a friendly tease
and desire a dream of you
and the shindig you disrupt
The generation that took cracks in the stoop
to be the price of disbelief
Reschedule the ceremony on higher ground
Wear shoes the right color pink
I know I'm in chains but the order's concise
A headache and pleasant apparitions
that break the day tacky with languor

REALM

Not capable to see what will happen
Hosts come and go and you submit
Your past envisioned as wires and rivers
Like everyone else you wear your bloodline
only nothing makes you a darling
Between that and your short fuse
The sinews that convey touch
When the current drains off you
and every cell quivers on its stem
Now you know the spy, you know your value
The most forward parts of you sway
since the twilight they emerge from
is both night's and day's
They compound in irradiated fatigue
You are entitled to derelictions
Accept this condescension as universal
You are in a realm beyond ailments
All the light one can admit
when most visible are the utterly heartless
You are not born able to wheedle
I hope your ankle will be a relic
A floral name such as Lily
No use to pretend the day is maiden
All her senses disguise and quicken
at the feet of her own disciple

DEFINITIVE TARGETS

It starts with a snippet of hearsay
The translation of thigh to the speech of our time
The box I drop my complaint in is on fire
or maybe the wine explodes sunset
One arm shores up the luggage
I compute body parts with dye on them
They reconstitute and greet me in the courtyard
When you consider the slashes in canopies
Appealing, one defends her right to growl
A plot against all the definitive targets
This minute there is no room for you on the hill
She requests only clothes to leave the queue in
She turns to you with profuse eyebrows
Many insults try to pinch her features
Vigor of her lack greater than flaws
You can set your watch to midnight by it
Wake her at eight to restore her
Watch odds and ends creep across her floor
Something inside namely hazard
Her invisibility begins to molder on a bus
One trip after visiting the prison
I hate to menace you but here I come
The bend and the curve lead to straight city lines
Her time of night lends her merit
All her advantages of her own invention
Force radiating inwardly
Intimacy belies her courage
Dimness and sleeping smells to watch over

REQUITAL

Always recall the sun is very very large
Central thing reduced by distance
Constant enough that I remain standing
Light is faint and there is nothing here
I can't live in the shadow of prettiness
Power stakes beauty apart
I realize everything is requital

Vigor leaks in through a hole
Vertigo hits me with cold air
Afraid to choke in the game of dreams
A woman waits in the mausoleum
Spray of her words decorates
a beam of light
She doesn't know how much
that crown is worth
A quality of mockingbird about her
What color they will paint her
When she dies depends on
how quickly they forget
what you call paradise

WALKING UPHILL

Look, at least it ain't heartening
Lavender in mist at daybreak
Knits all the churches together
Slickness to the touch

As if walking uphill
Impossible things begin
Wrong person answers the phone
Walk in cloth softened by dew
Would have thought myself forgotten

All I have to offer
The thrill it would give me
Like warm air over cold water
Confetti drifts across ceiling
Pause in your breathing
That would be just like you
Lie in bed count out loud sleep

What you are trying to do
I open the window warily
No idea how my heart stops

REMEDY

You remember, we are down below
Very bright, everything vivid
Reward of the sleeper state
I grow without the one who leaves
Evening passes like creation
I look in unlikely places
The other side's behind me
Happens

How many stars per organist
An intruder is compatible
Still in her youth with secrets
Some kind of namelessness
Planets count but only one matters

Remedy the exposed side
Rag doll rolls off pillow
Hips butt and thighs packed tight
Your daughter like a mountain spring
High up above my eyes

TO GET STREETLIGHT

In whose pocket
Scent of currency
Corner milling around
Doesn't mean this is
the evening you want

To get streetlight on film
Every twenty feet deeper
in the park green grays
After gray comes not
black and is full

Cadillac misses me first
Then a Crown Vic
Trees first I saw
inside fences
hang over the street
Under, cool dark is cold
Someone up ahead breaks
into the light
All along I thought
that would be me

GET HELP

Land should never slide
Waters dance so massively
There is no respite
Clouds high thick and cold
I inform you, of all people

Still a lot of smoke
Can't say I'm innocent
Get help with the transmission
Meanwhile, how to stay warm
What the neighborhood does

It isn't really haunting
Happens a second time
Perfectly clear face pale
Eye-catching plaid gloves
Apart from the weary

ACCENT GEOGRAPHY

Heavy hand
You only
half frozen
Shelf life mood
Bus too crowded

From far and wide
Accent geography
Faces to fish in

Confidence builds
strife and vice versa
Please some with
admiration
Wariness, alas

Everything else
is inattention

AFFINITY

Rocks part from their pebbles
Gloves separate from cheeks
Light folds
        into doorways
Path to a moor
           Revert to foam

I insist eventfully
You await emphasis
Promote me
        above affinity
I would never
          protest ornaments

This otherness has grown
onto us from the earth
If you all
        hear the supreme
Artificial sky opens
          You an island in it

THE SIGNS

Not easy to summarize
Entire summer, in fact
Lovely face, sweat beads

Maybe gifted in crowds
You read all the signs
Stop ten feet short

Check budget for warm affect
Hey you, with the plate
Must seek teen empress transfer

Exposed skin intimate *au deux*
Air dirty and breathable
I wait for your name

ONE PERCENT

They think nothing
matters in darkness
Card between fingers
Felt on tables, walls, heads
Stand up carefully
See without looking

You have jangles or not
Engine warms nerves cool
Only one percent truly knows
Naked trees humming wind
Short change embarrasses
I can tell "pregnant with"

All that you're after
Create your own fairest
Deep reservoir flow
Impossible to say
I will never roam far
One need of many to sleep

HAND SHY

Suggest rather than decide
Don't trust depictions of life
You are one hand shy

Broken the worst possible place
Pain itself your certification
Ever more alive at least

Already said, myself I'm small
To be honest, it's the crowd
Fit to wear nothing there

Boogie-woogie has to pause
Nobody that friendly is sober
No smoky curtains for luck

Remember last blues I looked into
Something unsettling and invaluable
Why I give my life airs

TRAIN MAYBE COMES

Train trembles still Brooklyn
I suspect the willies
Roll glass eye with my toe
Whole car eating from my hand
I invent yesterday
So wonderful so what

Chocolate key to the passion fruit lock
Shoe box below seat divested of labels
Eye catches mirroring surface
Unforgiving profile in brown
Lurid and American

Soft voices over rocking clanks
I change at a square
I debark to unusual animation
It's dark, has been for hours
I cling to black faces
I pass unnoticed

All day long and seldom at night
Electric tunnels, current drives
Part of every music I play
Bar closes, train maybe comes
I never meet you then

HOW TO DO WHAT

Waif on her way
The light presides
You cannot imagine

Grime to be excavated
The old or the dead
Less than half neon

Has to do what with hope
Oneself is adequate
Watch disappearances

Unseen and inaudible
An angel you dream
Escape not some but all

You get you see
Provide disappointment
Vivid parts tolerated

You demand to die
Best comes after
Nothing like life

TO GO ON

After a mother crawls into sleep
Aerosol night balmy and weird
She smiles throughout hallucinations

Rigged to lean on turns
Above her knee catches light
I listen for a voice of yours

Behind the drums I can't see you
Like there's a mike on my lapel
Friends steadily divide

Had only advice to go on
I consider, then again wander
Tedium perfused with lewd streets

Time goes by breast-feeding
Daylight without zing to it
Recover minutes later, miles away

OVER YOUR HEELS

Colors that don't appear on streets
Odors that rise from underground rivers
and descend on me like a crew of angels

I walk beside the woman
There is an enhancement
but she does not know me
I watch her fade away

I think too much of victims
I estimate my own luck too high
Sleep half the night on a sofa
You will be glad to dine with children

and walk as through leafless forest
Patter patter rain lips
footsteps and fingertips
Patter patter for the attentive

Seek how low the level
Go under the stick
Shoulders over your heels
Maybe somebody claps
That's the way you are

I tear through a wall of newsprint
tall as a tenement
Interviews flutter and opinions whip
in a wind that weathers normalcy
Reports of children who so seldom dine
you read their stories right through them

I have no purpose at last
and put myself to use

TAKE MY EYES

Couldn't take my eyes
Sand in your hair
Another planet

Watch and chain
All I want is less
You see my back

Bricks wet still hot
Narrow straight nose
The door descends

Bus window moony side
Look and look
I do not seek

I see you are back
You go to the very end
Place without a world

BONES

Listen to voices in my fingertips
To know all your nicknames
And that's probably what saved me

I am just as vacant, I'm never famished

Smallness upright, losing on third try
Enormous rocks for enormous holes

Where the river isn't and you die
No one lives for auctions
Get big at the expense of a felon

Used up candles in fantasies
A fake river on this train
Countless languages eliminate many

I spit blue on my hands nothing breaks
Pandemonium— funny losing you here
By streetlight as by moonlight

An example is diamonds, or bones